Introduction

Let's face it. People we can trust are hard to find. Ask any businessman and he'll tell you that good personnel is one of his greatest needs—and rarest discoveries. The same is true in the political arena. Or the church, for that matter. Such terms as "rip-off" and "phony" and "con artist" are commonly used against a leader or some so-called "public servant."

What's missing? Integrity.

We seldom even hear the term anymore. As a result, we are becoming increasingly more suspicious, less trusting . . . fearful of those who once received our full support.

But trust is something we must earn. Not being an automatic virtue, it is solid, authentic character learned and earned in the trenches of life, in the crucible of pressure. That's what this booklet is all about. If you genuinely desire to be different—part of the answer rather than part of the problem—in our dishonest and deceitful world, you will be encouraged by these words.

You *can* become one of those hard-to-find individuals we can trust.

Charles R. Swindoll

Integrity

It seemed good to Darius to appoint 120 satraps over the kingdom, that they should be in charge of the whole kingdom,

and over them three commissioners (of whom Daniel was one), that these satraps might be accountable to them, and that the king might not suffer loss.

Then this Daniel began distinguishing himself among the commissioners and satraps because he possessed an extraordinary spirit, and the king planned to appoint him over the entire kingdom.

Then the commissioners and satraps began trying to find a ground of accusation against Daniel in regard to government affairs; but they could find no ground of accusation or evidence of corruption, inasmuch as he was faithful, and no negligence or corruption was to be found in him.

Then these men said, "We shall not find any ground of accusation against this Daniel unless we find it against him with regard to the law of his God."

Then these commissioners and satraps came by agreement to the king and spoke to him as follows: "King Darius, live forever!

"All the commissioners of the kingdom, the prefects and the satraps, the high officials and the governors have consulted together that the king should establish a statute and enforce an injunction that anyone who makes a petition to any god or man besides you, O king, for thirty days, shall be cast into the lions' den.

"Now, O king, establish the injunction and sign the document so that it may not be changed, according to the law of the Medes and Persians, which may not be revoked."

Therefore King Darius signed the document, that is, the injunction.

Now when Daniel knew that the document was signed, he entered his house (now in his roof chamber he had windows open toward Jerusalem); and he continued kneeling on his knees three times a day, praying and giving thanks before his God, as he had been doing previously.

Then these men came by agreement and found Daniel making petition and supplication before his God.

Then they approached and spoke before the king about the king's injunction, "Did you not sign an injunction that any man who makes a petition to any god or man besides you, O king, for thirty days, is to be cast into the lions' den?" The king

*answered and said, "The statement is
true, according to the law of the Medes
and Persians, which may not be revoked."*

*Then they answered and spoke before
the king, "Daniel, who is one of the exiles
from Judah, pays no attention to you,
O king, or to the injunction which you
signed, but keeps making his petition
three times a day."*

*Then, as soon as the king heard this
statement, he was deeply distressed and
set his mind on delivering Daniel; and
even until sunset he kept exerting himself
to rescue him.*

*Then these men came by agreement to
the king and said to the king, "Recognize,
O king, that it is a law of the Medes and
Persians that no injunction or statute
which the king establishes may be
changed."*

*Then the king gave orders, and Daniel
was brought in and cast into the lions'
den. The king spoke and said to Daniel,
"Your God whom you constantly serve will
Himself deliver you"* (Daniel 6:1-16).

A Very Familiar Story

There are some stories in the
Bible that are so familiar we have given them
titles. These titles are so familiar, even a part of
that title is all we need to complete it. For ex-
ample:

"Noah and ＿＿＿＿ ＿＿＿＿."
"The Ark," sure.
Good! Then there's "David and ＿＿＿＿."
"Goliath."

All right, let's try some more: "Jonah and ___
___."

"The Whale."

"The Patience of ___."

"The Patience of Job."

"Moses Crossing" what?

Why, "the Red Sea," of course.

The "Destruction of Sodom and ___."

"Gomorrah" is the place.

One more, how about "Daniel and ___ ___
___."

I'm sure you thought, "the Lions' Den." Now, I find that a very interesting title.

The book of Daniel has twelve good-sized chapters filled with events, stories, and vast prophetic scenes. But, to the public, the most familiar topic in all the book is "Daniel and the Lions' Den."

I remember, as a little boy in Sunday school (when they kept me quiet enough to listen), hearing the story of "Daniel and the Lions' Den." Two things always bothered me as a kid. First, who threw old Daniel in a dangerous place like that, and second, what had he done that was so bad that they put him in a dungeon where the king of the jungle lived? One of the reasons I was curious about all that was because I did not want to wind up there myself!

As I got older and began to study the story for myself, I was surprised. I found out that Daniel was not in the lions' den because he had done something *wrong*, but because he had done something *right*. That confused me all the more! As a matter of fact, it still confuses many Christians today. We are under the impression that when we do what is wrong, we will be punished for it; but, when we do what is *right*, we will be rewarded for it soon afterwards. Now that makes good, logical, common sense . . . but, *it isn't always true.* Sometimes, when you do things wrong, you are rewarded for it (as far as this world is concerned); and occasionally, when you do what is *right*, you pay a terrible price for it. Invariably, that throws us a curve.

I had a man come to me following a morning worship service in our church in Fullerton, California, and share with me how he had done what was right on his job. He had diligently done his work. As a man of strong conviction, he stood by his guns, believing what he was doing was right. He had been both careful and consistent to do all this with wisdom. But, the very next Monday morning, he faced the threat of losing his job because of doing what was right. As a matter of fact, the following day he *did* lose his job.

That was his "lions' den," so to speak. Daniel was certainly not the last man to suffer for doing what is right.

Darius' Search for Integrity

Let's turn to Daniel 6 . . . the lions'-den chapter. But our interest will be on what happened *before* Daniel was dumped into the dungeon.

This chapter revolves around the decision of an exceedingly powerful man named Darius, the 62-year-old king, the man to whom Daniel answered. Notice the first verse of Daniel 6.

It seemed good to Darius to appoint 120 satraps . . . ."

We don't know what "satraps" means, because we do not use the term today. Some translations have rendered it "overseers." These were 120 men who shared Darius' delegation of authority over his kingdom. They were governmental officials who served under the king in charge of large sections of the kingdom. Darius set up 120 "overseers" to whom he delegated some of the authority of his responsibility. However, as soon as authority is delegated, a king runs the risk of corruption, and that's *exactly* what Darius feared, so he placed over those "satraps" an upper echelon. They were called "commissioners." Look at the verses with me.

It seemed good to Darius to appoint 120 satraps over the kingdom, that they should be in charge of the whole kingdom, and over them three commissioners (of whom Daniel was one), that these satraps might be accountable to them, and that the king might not suffer loss (Daniel 6:1-2).

The commissioners were responsible for the activity of the overseers. Daniel was one of the three commissioners (verse 2). This accountability arrangement was set up so the king would not suffer loss. The second verse clearly states that fact. It was to guard against financial rip-offs, quite frankly. Those 120 overseers or governors could otherwise make off with a lot of illegal revenue and get away with all sorts of illegal acts if they were not kept accountable.

And so these three men, who were apparently the most trusted in the kingdom, were given authority over the whole kingdom. What a responsible position Daniel held! He was, by this time, in his eighties. Even though in his eighties, Daniel wasn't shelved. He wasn't a useless, retired, dust-collecting, rocking-chair type. He was involved. (Was he ever!) He not only had seniority, he had superiority over many others. Look at verse 3.

Then this Daniel began distinguishing himself among the commissioners and satraps because he possessed an extraordinary spirit, and the king planned to appoint him over the entire kingdom (Daniel 6:3).

Daniel's Integrity —
The Marks of Godliness

Now, I want you to study verse 3 very carefully. In our world, it's not what you know, it's *who* you know that usually brings about a promotion. But in God's world, it's what you *are*, not who you know. It's what you are in your character. God saw fit, because of the marks of godliness—the integrity in Daniel's life—to move in the heart of King Darius to plan a promotion. Notice his extraordinary spirit. The Berkeley Version of the Bible calls it a "surpassing spirit."

Our tendency is to think in terms of the spiritual life—that he was a spirit-filled man. That's true, but I don't take it to mean just that here in verse 3. I take it to refer to his *attitude*.

An Excellent Attitude

The first mark of godliness in the life of Daniel was an excellent attitude. Now, if you want to be a person of integrity, you must begin down deep within. With your attitude. It's so easy to mask our lives and look as though our attitude is good when in reality it isn't. One of the first places it shows up is in the realm of our work.

It's significant that there was no jealousy in Daniel's heart against those other two men who were appointed as commissioners. He could have been threatened, he could have been competitive, he could have been rather nasty and ugly in his responsibilities, because he had the longest time in the kingdom. Long before those men had even come upon the scene, he had been in authority under previous monarchs. But, because he possessed that "extraordinary spirit," the king planned to appoint him over the entire kingdom.

Let me pause right here and ask you about *your* attitude. How is it? Perhaps it's good right now, but what about tomorrow morning when you punch in on the time clock? Or what about by the end of the day tomorrow evening? How will your eight to ten hours have been? As you work shoulder to shoulder with people in your shop, in your office, or among the sales force where you are employed, or in the secretarial pool, what kind of attitude will you have? An excellent attitude means so much!

You might wonder, "Will my boss notice if I have a good attitude?" Don't worry about that. He'll stumble all over it! He'll be amazed by it. In fact, he'll be *terribly* impressed. Maybe I should warn you ahead of time—your trouble won't come from your employer. Your main troubles will come from your fellow workers, who are often lazy and dishonest and bothered that you're not like them. And because you won't be like they are, you will discover they will become envious and jealous and so petty that you might even begin to endure what Daniel experienced.

Read on and you'll see that's exactly what happened. Look at the plot that took place against our 80-year-old friend. First, there were attempted accusations:

> *Then the commissioners* (that is, the other two—Daniel's peers) *and the satraps began trying to find a ground of accusation against Daniel in regard to government affairs* . . . (Daniel 6:4).

Now, isn't that significant? Here's a man who was doing a splendid job, who had an excellent attitude, and who was apparently working very hard for his superior and among his peers. And yet those who were working around him and under him set up a spying program against him. They began to search for something they could use as accusations against him. It says they searched in the realm of "government affairs." And what did they find? Well, verse 4 continues:

> . . . *they could find no ground of accusation or evidence of corruption.* . . .

Wow! How would you like *your* work to come under that kind of close scrutiny? I mean, out there where you make a living—not the way you are on Sunday, but the way you are where you earn your living. How would you make out if for some reason a group of secret investigators began to examine your work? What would they find? Would it make you nervous? Would you have to burn or destroy some evidence? Or hide some of the skeletons you have tucked away in the closet? Daniel was investigated to see if they could find *anything* with regard to his work—that's government affairs—in the realm of occupation. And the remarkable thing is that they could not find one ground of accusation. They could not find one shred of damaging evidence . . . no corruption! That's not only remarkable, today it seems impossible.

Some of us are going through a time of real rethinking about our total trust in government. We who love this country and love it dearly (and would fight to the last day to preserve it) are becoming increasingly more concerned about integrity at the higher levels of our government. I think it speaks with immediate relevance when it says that Daniel was not found guilty of any accusation or corruption.

Faithful in His Work

Here is the second mark of godliness: he was faithful in his work. Now, be careful here. We often use the word faithful only as it relates to the spiritual life, the religious life. But it's not talking about faithfulness at church or in the temple, as if referring to worship. They are investigating *his occupation*. They are looking for something they could criticize in his faithfulness at work. This passage says that when Daniel was investigated, he was found to be faithful in his work. There was an absence of negligence. The Berkeley Version of the Bible says he was faithful "in the discharge of his official duties" (Daniel 6:4).

Look at Proverbs 20:6-7. Verse 6 reads:

*Many a man proclaims his own loyalty,
but who can find a trustworthy man?*

It's asked with the answer in mind. It's rare. Only on very few occasions will you find an individual who is completely trustworthy. I had a man tell me recently that in his business it isn't the public that gives him trouble; it's his employees. It isn't just the public that steals his goods; it's often those who work for him. It has come to the place where many an employer will no longer hire a Christian! As a matter of fact, when we were living in Texas, we were close friends with the president of a bank, and the highest risk for bank loans were preachers! Isn't that significant? Those who gave him the most difficulty were those who were engaged continually in the ministry of God's Word.

It's time again to appraise your personal life. Are you trustworthy? Can others count on you to get the job done when the boss isn't around? Are you a faithful employee?

Verse 7 goes on to say:

A righteous man who walks in his integrity—how blessed are his sons after him.

A righteous man walks where? He walks in his *integrity*. Now, that's what Daniel 6 is talking about. Daniel was faithful in his work. There was no negligence, no corruption found in him. What a man! Faithful in his work.

Personal Purity

I find in the last part of verse 4 yet another mark of godliness: personal purity. A life of purity that can stand up under the most intense scrutiny. Today, we would say that they "tailed" him. They followed him, spied on him, searched through his personal effects, and they discovered after that examination that there was nothing lacking. No hanky-panky. No hidden dirt. Zero! He was a man of personal purity. They could dig all they wished and Daniel came out smelling like a rose.

Wouldn't you love to hire a person like that? Wouldn't that be great? I am continually hearing from employers that their number one problem is personnel; that is, finding trustworthy personnel. I mean through and through.

Some time ago, I heard about a fellow in Long Beach who went into a fried chicken place to get some chicken for himself and the young lady he was with. She waited in the car while he went in to pick up the chicken. Inadvertently, the manager of the store handed the guy the box in which he had placed the proceeds of the day instead of the box of chicken. You see, he was going to make a deposit and had camouflaged it by putting the money in a fried chicken box.

The fellow took his box, went back to the car, and the two of them drove away. When they got to the park and opened the box, they discovered they had a box full of money. Now that's a very vulnerable moment for the average individual. He realized there must have been a mistake, so he got back in the car and drove back to the place and gave the money back to the manager. Well, the manager was elated! He was so pleased that he told the young man, "Stick around, I want to call the newspaper and have them put your picture in it. You're the most honest guy in town."

"Oh, no, don't do that!" said the fellow.

"Why not?" asked the manager.

"Well," he said, "you see, I'm married, and the woman I'm with is not my wife!"

Now, I think that is a perfect illustration of how *on the surface* we may look like people of honesty and great integrity. It looks like others can count on folks to be so thoroughly honest they'd give the dime back at the phone booth . . . but underneath, it isn't unusual to find a lot of corruption there.

Not Daniel! They found he was incredible—an excellent attitude, faithfully doing his job at work, an honest man who was personally pure. No hypocrisy. Nothing to hide.

Now, that so frustrated those who were investigating him that verse 5 tells us they set up a devastating plan. After their earlier plot began to run its course and they couldn't find an accusation, they then determined to do something worse. They would have an injunction written against him.

Notice how they appealed to the vanity of the king.

> Then these men said, "We shall not find
> any ground of accusation against this
> Daniel unless we find it against him with
> regard to the law of his God" (Daniel 6:5).

One thing they had discovered about Daniel when they investigated him was that he was a man of God. They said, "Look, this man is so consistent in his walk that the only place we're going to trip him up is to use his faith in God against him." Go on to the next verse:

> *Then these commissioners and*
> *satraps came by agreement to the king . . .*
> (Daniel 6:6).

Interesting, "by agreement." It was all a conspiracy. It was a well-planned program to sell Daniel down the river. Then they appealed to the vanity of the king.

> *"King Darius, live forever! All the*
> *commissioners of the kingdom . . . have*
> *consulted together. . . .*

Wait a minute! That's a lie!! All but *one* of the commissioners of the kingdom. Daniel didn't know anything about it, but they acted as though Daniel was part of this plan. Here's the way it reads:

> *All the commissioners of the kingdom,*
> *the prefects and the satraps, the high*
> *officials and the governors have consulted*
> *together that the king should establish a*
> *statute and enforce an injunction that*
> *anyone who makes a petition to any god*
> *or man besides you, O king, for thirty*
> *days, shall be cast into the lions' den*
> (Daniel 6:7).

Now, *that* is the basis of the lions' den. By the way, they didn't want to throw him in a fiery furnace because they were Zoroastrians by faith. That religion believed fire to be sacred, and to have cremated him would have been to make a god out of him. So many who dedicated their living being to fire did it as a worship to the gods. They didn't want to put him into a fire, because that would be worshipping their god through that sacrifice. So they said, "Let's put into a den of lions anyone who doesn't worship Darius for thirty days." How interesting.

Many years ago, there was a program on television entitled, "Queen for a Day." You may remember that the lady who won got top treatment for that entire day! Well, in this case, they were suggesting that Darius be made "God of the Month"! That's exactly what they said. "For these thirty days, if anybody worships anyone else but you, O king, they will be thrown into the lions' den." How flatteringly cruel!

> "Now, O king, establish the injunction
> and sign the document so that it may not
> be changed, according to the law of the
> Medes and Persians . . ." (Daniel 6:8).

We have that same phrase today. You know how it goes: "the law of the Medes and Persians"—it will never be changed.

> ". . . which may not be revoked." There-
> fore King Darius signed the document. . . .

That is, the injunction. Darius thought it was a great idea. Naturally, he would. Now what happens? Don't forget that our man Daniel isn't deserving of *any* of this. This sneaky conspiracy against him was because he had done what was right, remember? Now, verse 10:

> When Daniel knew that the document
> was signed. . . .

That's significant. He knew nothing of it until the document was signed. Dirty deal! Not only had they tried raking through his life to find some slip-up in his service record, but they concocted a law that Daniel's honest and pure life style would automatically violate. And they did it behind his back. Some reward for having nothing to hide!

Consistent Walk with God

But suddenly we learn what Daniel did when he heard that the document was signed.

Now when Daniel knew that the document was signed, he entered his house (now in his roof chamber he had windows open toward Jerusalem); and he continued kneeling on his knees three times a day, praying and giving thanks before his God, as he had been doing previously (Daniel 6:10).

I submit to you, that's an incredible response to one's own death warrant. I find here his fourth mark of godliness—his consistent walk with God.

I think the last part of that verse is the most remarkable:

. . . as he had been doing previously.

Daniel did not turn to prayer in panic. He had been consistently on his knees three times a day before his God, day in, day out, year after year. By the way, remember, he was one of the top officials in the land, yet he had time with God regularly. The psalmist writes:

Evening, and morning, and at noon, will I pray, and cry aloud: and he shall hear my voice (Psalm 55:17, KJV).

Isn't that a great verse? Evening, morning, noon, I will pray. Daniel was no stranger to prayer. But still he didn't flaunt the fact that he was a man of prayer. Notice his windows were *already* open. He didn't suddenly bang them open so that everyone would know he was praying and be impressed with his piety.

There was an advertisement some time ago from one of the airlines. It said, "When you've got it, flaunt it." That may work for an airline, but it doesn't work for an authentic man or woman of God. When you've got it, you *don't* flaunt it. Why? Because when you flaunt it, you really don't have it.

Daniel just quietly walked up to the chamber in his home and again before God he poured out his fear, his concern, his future, his life. Daniel is phenomenal. Just very near unreal. We Christians have a low threshold of pain, don't we? When things run along pretty well, we can stay fairly consistent; but a little ripple comes in the water, and we plunge! We pray at those times, but they are usually panic prayers, "Help-me-out-of-this-mess" prayers. Not Daniel! The remarkable thing about him is that he simply went back to God as before. I think if they had had an electrocardiogram, it would read just the same as always, like those astronauts of years gone by. Just before the blast off, scientists and medical specialists did that test on them and it was just like the morning before when they were having breakfast. "What else is new? Going around the earth, ho hum." And off they went.

And Daniel? "Well, what else is new? What do you expect from the world?" So he heard about this news and he just went right back to God and told God about them. He had a place to meet. By the way, will you observe that he got on his knees. I want to suggest that kneeling is a good way to pray, because it's *uncomfortable.* Our problem is that we pray in such a comfortable position that we just sort of drift off after a few sentences. Try that. Jim Elliot has said:

God is still on His throne and man is still on his footstool. There's only a knee's distance in between.

How is *your* time in prayer? What does it take to get you on your knees? A tragedy? A real emergency? This man had been doing this as a habit of his life. He had a place to meet with God and he met. He consistently kept his life and his burdens at the throne. Please don't excuse yourself because you're too busy. Not a person reading this page is busier than Daniel could have been as one of the three top men in the country. You can't get busier than that. But somehow, his consistent walk with God was so important, he simply stayed before His presence. I don't think he spent hours there, but I think he spent significant periods of time just punctuating his needs of the day, week in and week out.

Integrity: How to Develop It

Let's review the marks of Daniel's godliness: He had an excellent attitude. He was faithful at work. He maintained a high level of personal purity. He had a consistent walk with God.

The public arrest came as the result of that godly life.

Then these men came by agreement and found Daniel making petition and supplication before his God (Daniel 6:11).

Isn't that significant? They interrupted him in prayer. That's where they found him "doing wrong." And the final result? The lions' den, that's what.

> Then the king gave orders, and Daniel was brought in and cast into the lions' den (Daniel 6:16a).

How about that? A more godly influence could not be found in the entire kingdom of Persia, and he was the man who was thrown into the lions' den. A man with four great marks of godliness was dumped into the dungeon.

Let me share with you three lessons that I have learned as we wrap up our thoughts on this passage. The first one is this: *You will seldom get what you deserve from people, so don't expect it.* That applies to both criticism and honor. When you are genuinely deserving of honor, you will seldom get it from people; and when you are genuinely deserving of criticism, you will seldom get it as you should. You will seldom get direct confrontation at the time you need it. Usually, when you do receive it, you'll get it at the wrong time. When the world administers its reproach, it's frequently wrong. You'll get promoted when you don't deserve it. You'll even get demoted when it isn't fair. You'll seldom get what you deserve from people, so don't expect it. Perhaps because Daniel knew this, he wasn't blown away when his enemies accused him.

Second, *you will always get what is best from God, so don't doubt it.* The interesting thing about it is that it won't come in the package you expect and it usually will be delivered late according to your timing expectations. God plans His best for us . . . and then He delivers it according to His time scale.

You'll seldom get what you deserve from people. Don't expect it.

You will always get what is best from God. Don't doubt it, even though it may come slowly.

Here's the third: *Your ability to handle both is directly related to the consistency of your walk with the Lord.* And that's the crux of this entire little booklet. Daniel could handle the final blow, because he had been consistently walking with God. You cannot handle the honors nor can you handle the attacks if your walk with God is inconsistent. You will begin to think you really are deserving of honor or you will begin to doubt in the midst of a trial because you think you are deserving of something else.

Dr. Ralph Byron is one of the most interesting and outstanding Christian surgeons in the Los Angeles area. Early in his medical profession he sought for a way to make life count. Professionally and personally, he wanted to be a man of God. One day in his search for godliness, he came across Ezekiel 22:30

And I searched for a man among them who should build up the wall and stand in the gap before Me for the land, that I should not destroy it; but I found no one.

Dr. Byron pondered this kind of question: "Would God find me standing in the gap?" Here he was a young surgeon with the press of responsibility all around him, and he answered the question honestly, "No, not right now." He concluded that in order for him to be a man of God, he must continually place a priority on prayer.

At first, it was very difficult, because his duties were numerous. He decided that in order for him to have time with God, he would personally have to get up very early. He set aside the time of 5:30 a.m., which he called "an unearthly hour." But he did it. It was the best time, in light of his busy schedule. Week after week. The remarkable thing he discovered was that within just two weeks, he began to have a quality of life he had never known before. He saw two men trust Christ. He discovered that a major conflict in their church had been resolved—dissolved is a better word—as he committed it faithfully to God in prayer. And so he concluded, "It was apparent to me that I must give prayer top priority, even if it means getting less than six hours of sleep every night."

Now, I'm not demanding, necessarily, that you get up at 5:00 or 5:30 every morning. Some of us function a lot better later on and are a lot more effective when we are wide awake. It's not the time of day that's important, it's that *there is a top priority every day for God.* That's what this is all about. We don't read that Daniel got up at 3:00 in the morning and prayed until daybreak. We just read that he prayed three times a day. There was a priority for prayer in his life.

If the truth were known, in many of our lives, there is not that priority, and I freely confess that it has not been on a number of occasions in my own life. At one of those "low tide" experiences in my life, I saw this quotation hanging on a wall:

> *When you're faced with a busy day, save precious time by skipping your devotions.*
> *Signed, Satan.*

That's what some of you have done, isn't it? That's why you are very relieved to know it was Daniel who was placed into the lions' den and not you, right?

Have you come to the place in your life where you are not getting what you deserve from people? If the truth were known, some of you could say, "That's the story of my life. I have been misunderstood; I have been misused; I have been wrongly criticized."

It's time to take account of God's hand in your life. Some of you have begun to doubt it. Some of you have begun to let the busy day crowd out your time with God. You can't remember the last time you had a meaningful encounter on your knees, apart from an emergency. No wonder you're having trouble with relationships! No wonder your attitude is poor at work! No wonder you're suffering from this emptiness of heart at home, at work, within yourself!

Daniel had no corner on integrity. The marks of godliness are available to you. Make plans to meet with God. Don't announce it, just do it. Be consistent. Watch it work.

Lord God, help us be people who consistently walk with You. Strengthen us as we trust in You and lean on You when the cares of the world around us cave in and would otherwise crush us. Thank you, dear Father, for our Savior Jesus Christ, who understands and assists us in our deepest needs.

We pray in His strong name. Amen.